REAL TALK
4 TEENAGERS

REAL TALK
4 TEENAGERS

K. R. WALKER

Tampa, Florida

Real Talk 4 Teenagers

Published by Gatekeeper Press
7853 Gunn Hwy, Suite 209
Tampa, FL 33626
www.GatekeeperPress.com

Scripture quotations taken from the Holy Bible, KJV.

Copyright © 2024 K. R. Walker, all rights reserved. No part of this book may be reproduced or transmitted in any form or by any means, electronic or mechanical, including photocopying, recording or by any information storage and retrieval system without written permission from the author.

This publication is designed to provide accurate and authoritative information in regard to the subject matter covered. It is sold with the understanding that the publisher is not engaged in rendering legal or accounting services. If legal advice or other expert assistance is required, the services of a competent professional person should be sought.

ISBN: 9781662956119

Special Thank You to Y I Believe For Supporting
This Book. Subscribe to: www.yibelieveproject.com

We invite you to share your thoughts on Real Talk 4 Teenagers. Enter to win a gift card!

Realtalk4walker@gmail.com

Printed in the United States of America

CONTENTS

1. Building Self-Esteem and Confidence 1
2. Finding Your Passion 3
3. Staying True to Yourself 6
4. Developing Resilience 9
5. Time Management Skills for High School Students 11
6. Balancing School and Extracurricular Activities 13
7. Preparing for College 15
8. Making Friends and Building Healthy Relationships 18
9. Talk So People Can Listen 20
10. Understanding Consent and Respect in Relationships 22
11. Navigating Social Media Safely and Responsibly 24
12. Guide on Teenagers Dating 26

13. Communication Skills 28
14. Exploring Career Options 30
15. Finding the Right Path for You 32
16. Resume and Job Interview 34
17. Guide on Financial Literacy 36
18. Managing Your Money 38
19. Guide for Writing a Business Plan for Teens 40
20. Guide for Teen Investing 42
21. Healthy Eating Habits for Busy Teens 44
22. The Importance of Exercise 46
23. Understanding Puberty and Body Changes 48
24. Getting Enough Rest Is Necessary 50
25. How to Navigate the Teenage Years 52
26. How to Avoid Getting Sick 54
27. Hygiene Is Important 56
28. What Girls Can Expect During Their Menstrual Cycle 58
29. How to Manage Stress Effectively 60
30. Dealing with Peer Pressure 62
31. How Teenagers Can Deal With Cyberbullying 64
32. Basic Cooking Skills Every Teen Should Learn 66
33. Creating Your Own Space 68
34. How to Keep the Environment Safe and Clean 70

35. Heal from the Death of a Loved One 72
36. Mending a Broken Heart 74
37. Teenagers Responsibility Towards Adults 76
38. Driving Safety Tips For New Drivers 78
39. What You Need to Know About Credit 81
40. Guide for Applying for Grants for Colleges 83
41. Reasons You Should Not Purchase or
    Play with Guns 85
42. Reasons You Should Not Do Drugs,
    Alcohol, or Join Gangs 87
43. What to Expect After High School and
    Choices to Consider 89
44. What to Do When You are Pulled Over
    by a Police Officer 92
45. Senses on a Spiritual Level 94
46. What the Bible say to Children 97
47. Spiritual Guidance 99
48. Encouraging and Empowering
    Teens Worldwide 101
49. Be Prepared And Armor Yourself 103
50. How God Communicates with You 105
51. Who is God 107
52. What God Wants Teens to Know 109
53. Message to Teens from God 111

54. The Importance of Prayer 113
55. Evening Prayers 114
56. Devotional Prayers 115
57. Walking In The Fruits of the Spirit 116

Acknowledgement 118
To My Mother 120
Advice from the Author 122
The Prayer 124

BUILDING SELF-ESTEEM AND CONFIDENCE

Understand that your worth is not tied to your achievements, grades, or social status. You are valuable just as you are. Embrace self-love by accepting yourself, including your flaws and imperfections. Believe that you can improve and grow through effort and learning. Understand that abilities are not fixed but can be developed over time. Recognize that mistakes are part of the learning process. Instead of seeing failure as a reflection of your worth, view it as an opportunity to learn and grow. Focus on the effort and hard work you put into tasks rather than just the outcomes. Celebrate milestones by acknowledging the perseverance and dedication it took to achieve them. Identify areas where you struggle and see them as opportunities for growth. Engage in activities that build on your passions and interests, which can help you develop new skills and boost self-esteem. Choose friends who lift you up and make you feel good about yourself.

Avoid people who bring negativity into your life or make you feel inadequate. Pay attention to the voice in your head and challenge negative thoughts. Replace self-critical thoughts with positive affirmations that are true, fair, and kind. Understand that nobody is perfect, and striving for perfection can hinder self-esteem. Do your best in everything but accept that making mistakes is part of being human. Set achievable goals for yourself and work towards them step by step. Celebrate small victories along the way to build confidence in your abilities. Don't hesitate to ask for help from trusted adults like parents or teachers when you're struggling with low self-esteem or other challenges.

FINDING YOUR PASSION

Finding your passion can be an exciting yet difficult journey. It's important to remember that discovering what you love takes time and exploration. Start by identifying what interests you. Think about activities that make you feel excited or engaged. What do you enjoy doing in your free time? This could be anything from playing sports, painting, writing, coding, or playing an instrument. Which subjects do you find most intriguing at school? Are there topics that spark your curiosity? Participate in various extracurricular activities like clubs, sports teams, or volunteer opportunities to see what resonates with you. Reflecting on your thoughts and feelings can provide clarity. Here are some questions to consider: What projects or hobbies make you lose track of time? If money were no object, what career would you choose? What kind of impact do you want to have on the world? Who do you admire and why? Don't be afraid to step out of your comfort zone! Trying new experiences can lead to unexpected passions. Sign up for workshops or classes in areas you've never explored before—like cooking, photography, or coding. Get involved in community service projects. This not only helps others but also exposes you to different fields and perspectives. Seek internships or part-time jobs related to your interests. Real-world experience can help clarify what you enjoy. After trying different activities, take time to reflect on them. What did you enjoy most about each experience? Were there any challenges that excited you rather than discouraged you? Did any activity make you feel proud of yourself? Engage with people who share similar interests or who work in fields you're curious about. Find a mentor who can guide and support your exploration process. Attend events where professionals gather; this could include workshops, seminars, or local meetups. Understand that passions can evolve over time. It's okay if something that once excited you no longer does, allow yourself the freedom to change paths. Be open-minded about new interests as they arise. Visualizing your goals can help solidify your aspirations. Gather images, quotes, and words that resonate with your dreams. Arrange them on a board where you'll see it often as a reminder of what you're working towards. Once you've identified potential passions. Set specific goals related to those interests. Break these goals into actionable steps so they feel manageable. Acknowledge every step forward in your journey. Celebrate achievements—big or small—to build confidence and motivation. Finding your passion is a journey that requires patience. Don't rush the process; give yourself grace as you explore different avenues. Remember, it's perfectly normal not to have everything figured out right away! Just stay focus.

STAYING TRUE TO YOURSELF

Staying true to yourself is a vital aspect of leading a fulfilling and authentic life. It involves understanding your core values, embracing your individuality, and navigating social pressures while maintaining integrity. This guide will provide you with actionable steps to help you stay true to yourself in various aspects of life. Take time to reflect on what truly matters to you. Identify the principles that guide your decisions and actions. Consider making a list of characteristics or beliefs that resonate with you, such as honesty, compassion, creativity, or independence. Once you've identified your values, rank them in order of importance. This prioritization will serve as a compass for your decisions and interactions with others. Understanding your emotions is crucial for self-awareness. Regularly check in with yourself to acknowledge how you're feeling and why those feelings arise. Focus on what you excel at and what brings you joy. Engage in activities that align with your skills and passions, whether they are hobbies, professional pursuits, or interpersonal skills. Establish clear boundaries in both personal and professional relationships. Let others know what behaviors are acceptable and which ones are not. Practice saying no when asked to participate in activities that don't align with your values or interests. Remember that it's okay to prioritize your well-being over social expectations. Surround yourself with individuals who respect and encourage you for who you are. Positive relationships can reinforce your sense of self and provide support during challenging times. Find friends or mentors who can help hold you accountable for staying true to your values. They can offer guidance when you're faced with difficult decisions. Be open about your thoughts, feelings, and preferences without fear of judgment. Authentic expression fosters deeper connections with others. Acknowledge what makes you different from others, your experiences, perspectives, talents and you should take pride in those qualities. Learn not to internalize the negative judgments of others. Focus on constructive feedback from trusted sources while ignoring unjustified criticisms. Do not compare yourself to others just focus on your journey and growth as an individual. Treat yourself with the same kindness you would offer a close friend. Acknowledge that everyone makes mistakes, use them as opportunities for growth rather than reasons for self-criticism. Recognize that being vulnerable is a strength that can lead to deeper connections with others and greater self-acceptance. Set measurable and attainable goals aligned with your values and interests. This approach helps maintain focus on personal growth while staying true to yourself.

DEVELOPING RESILIENCE

Building resilience can help you navigate life's ups and downs more effectively. Resilience is not about being invulnerable or never feeling pain. It's about learning how to cope with difficulties and recover from setbacks. Think of it as developing internal strength rather than relying on external shields. Having at least one caring and supportive adult in your life can make a significant difference. This could be a parent, teacher, coach, or mentor. Friendships provide emotional support and a sense of belonging. Don't hesitate to ask for advice or help when you need it. Talk about your emotions with someone you trust. Mindfulness helps you stay present and manage stress. Take slow, deep breaths to calm yourself. A positive mindset can help you deal with challenges more effectively. Write down things you are grateful for each day. Replace negative thoughts with positive affirmations. Divide larger goals into smaller, manageable steps. Acknowledge your achievements along the way. Think of different ways to tackle an issue. Having strategies in place can help you manage stress better. Engage in activities that calm you, like listening to music or reading a book. Understanding that change is necessary and can make it easier to adapt. Be open to new experiences and changes in plans. Reflect on what each experience teaches you. If you focus on these areas, you'll build the resilience needed to face life's challenges head-on while growing stronger through each experience.

TIME MANAGEMENT SKILLS FOR HIGH SCHOOL STUDENTS

High school can be a busy time with academics, extracurricular activities, chores, and social life. Mastering time management skills is crucial to balance these responsibilities effectively. Time management involves using techniques to use your time more effectively. It includes prioritizing and organizing tasks based on their importance and urgency. By focusing on the most critical tasks first, you can make the best use of your energy and efforts. Create checklists and to-do lists. Set clear goals (daily, weekly, monthly). Determine priorities based on urgency and importance. Review and improve workflows regularly. Waking up earlier can help you take full advantage of the day. Ensure you get enough sleep by setting an early bedtime. Avoid multitasking as it can lead to distractions. Focus on one task at a time for better efficiency. Utilize apps designed for productivity but avoid getting distracted by social media notifications while working on assignments. Establish realistic deadlines for each task considering your workload and other commitments. Periodically review what you have accomplished versus what remains pending to adjust your plans accordingly. Finding motivation can be tough especially if you're uninterested in a subject or activity. Feeling overwhelmed by too many tasks can lead to abandoning them altogether. Develop a prioritized to-do list focusing on essential tasks first while postponing less critical ones if necessary. Getting more done in less time, reducing stress levels, preventing procrastination, improving decision-making skills.

BALANCING SCHOOL AND EXTRACURRICULAR ACTIVITIES

Balancing school and extracurricular activities can be challenging, but with the right strategies, it is entirely possible to excel in both areas. Here are some detailed tips to help you achieve a healthy balance. Your primary responsibility as a student is your academics. Prioritize your classes, assignments, and exams above everything. This doesn't mean neglecting extracurricular activities, but rather ensuring that your academic performance remains strong. Creating a detailed schedule is crucial for managing your time effectively. Plan out what needs to be done and when it needs to be finished. Prioritize your activities so you don't leave anything important for last. When scheduling, make sure to allocate sufficient time for studying before adding extracurriculars. Do not join every club or organization that's available . Instead, choose wisely among those you are truly interested in and those that will help you on your way to success. It is best to pick no more than three or four activities and focus on them through obtaining leadership positions. While aiming for high grades is important, overdoing it can lead to burnout. Study in segments of 45 minutes to an hour with a break of five to ten minutes in between. Use this time to stretch, recharge with a snack, or simply relax. Whether you're a procrastinator or hyper-organized type, planning ahead is essential for balancing school and extracurriculars effectively. Be realistic about what you can manage and communicate any conflicts with friends or teammates early on. Find a quiet place where you can focus without distractions, such as a library or designated study room. Turn off your phone and dedicate uninterrupted time to homework or studying. Set specific goals for yourself and reward yourself upon achieving them. For example, finish an assignment before allowing yourself some leisure time. If you have long commutes or waiting periods between activities, use this time productively by listening to audio versions of textbooks or recording yourself reading study materials aloud. Combine socializing with physical exercise by inviting friends for hikes, walks, workout classes, or gym sessions together. Understand that plans may change due to unforeseen circumstances like extra homework or rescheduled events. Prioritize your mental health and well-being alongside your commitments. If you follow these tips, you can create a balanced lifestyle that allows you to excel academically while still enjoying the benefits of extracurricular activity.

PREPARING FOR COLLEGE

1. Freshman Year

Outline the classes you want to take throughout high school. Include all required classes for graduation. Identify potential Honors and AP classes. Add some enjoyable classes to maintain interest. Develop an organizational system and stick to it. Complete assignments fully and turn them in on time. Practice note-taking skills using different methods. Manage your time effectively and efficiently. Explore where and how you study best. Join school clubs and extracurricular activities to explore interests. Engage in volunteer work and community service events. Build important life skills like teamwork, leadership, and time management. Keep a comprehensive list of activities, awards, jobs, internships, etc. Update your resume regularly to ensure accuracy.

2. Sophomore Year

Maintain a high GPA by continuing good study habits. Take more challenging courses if possible. Take elective courses that align with potential career interests. Attend career fairs or job shadowing opportunities. Familiarize yourself with the standardized tests like the SAT or ACT. Take on leadership roles in clubs or organizations. Continue participating in volunteer work and community service.

3. Junior Year

Register for the SAT or ACT and consider taking both to see which suits you better. Take advantage of test prep resources such as books, online courses, or tutoring. Start researching colleges that interest you based on location, size, programs offered, etc. Visit college campuses if possible to get a feel for the environment. Continue building your college resume with new activities, awards, jobs, internships, etc. Identify teachers or mentors who can write strong letters of recommendation for your college applications.

4. Senior Year

Narrow down your list of colleges to those you will apply to. Complete college applications paying close attention to deadlines. Write compelling personal statements or essays required by grants that you may be eligible for and apply. Practice interviewing skills if any of your chosen colleges require interviews as part of their application process. Continue working hard in your classes, senior year grades still matter. Studying effectively is crucial for academic success, especially as you transition from high school to college.

MAKING FRIENDS AND BUILDING HEALTHY RELATIONSHIPS

Friendships play a crucial role in our mental health and overall well-being. They can reduce stress, prevent loneliness, and provide support during tough times. Recognizing the significance of friendships is the first step in building healthy relationships. If you struggle with shyness or social awkwardness, remember that many people feel the same way. Focus on showing genuine interest in others, as this can help you connect more easily. Putting yourself out there and taking small steps to initiate conversations can gradually build your confidence. Explore various avenues to meet new people, such as volunteering, joining clubs or groups related to your interests, attending community events, or taking classes. These environments provide opportunities to interact with like-minded individuals and potentially form friendships. Making friends requires effort and initiative. Be proactive in reaching out to others, initiating conversations, and suggesting activities or outings. By taking the first step, you demonstrate your willingness to invest in the relationship. Effective communication is key to building strong relationships. Practice active listening by paying attention to what others say, showing empathy, and asking thoughtful questions. Being a good listener fosters trust and deepens connections with others. Maintaining friendships involves regular communication, spending quality time together, and offering support when needed. Make an effort to stay connected with your friends through calls, messages, or face-to-face interactions. Healthy relationships are built on mutual respect and understanding boundaries. It's important to communicate openly about your needs and expectations within the friendship while also respecting the boundaries set by others. Conflicts are a natural part of any relationship but addressing them in a constructive manner is essential for maintaining healthy friendships. Practice effective conflict resolution by expressing your feelings calmly, listening to the other person's perspective, and working towards finding a mutually acceptable solution. Sharing moments of joy and celebrating each other's achievements strengthens the bond between friends. Acknowledge milestones, offer encouragement, and be genuinely happy for your friends' accomplishments. Focus on cultivating meaningful connections rather than accumulating a large number of acquaintances. Quality friendships based on trust and mutual respect.

TALK SO PEOPLE CAN LISTEN

Teens should aim to communicate their thoughts and ideas clearly and concisely. Avoid rambling or going off on tangents, as this can make it difficult for listeners to follow along. Encourage teens to actively listen to the person they are speaking with. This means maintaining eye contact, nodding to show understanding, and asking relevant questions to demonstrate engagement. Teach teens how to express their emotions in a healthy and constructive manner. Encourage them to use "I" statements to convey their feelings without blaming others. Remind teens of the importance of letting others speak without interruption. Waiting for the other person to finish before responding shows respect and improves overall communication. Encourage teens to ask questions that promote further discussion rather than simple yes or no answers. This helps keep conversations flowing and engaging. Help teens develop empathy by considering the feelings and perspectives of others during conversations. Encouraging them to see things from different viewpoints fosters better communication. Remind teens that nonverbal cues such as facial expressions, gestures, and body language play a significant role in communication. Being mindful of these cues can enhance understanding between individuals. Encourage teens to seek feedback on their communication skills from trusted individuals. Constructive criticism can help them identify areas for improvement and grow as effective communicators.

UNDERSTANDING CONSENT AND RESPECT IN RELATIONSHIPS

It is a mutual agreement between participants to engage in a specific activity, based on clear communication and mutual respect. Consent should be straightforward and unambiguous, with explicit communication. Consent must be given freely without any form of coercion or pressure. Consent can be withdrawn at any time, emphasizing the importance of continuous communication and respect for changing decisions. Always ask before sharing someone's personal information. Seek permission before borrowing something from someone. Respect personal boundaries and seek consent before initiating physical contact. Always ask for permission before entering someone's personal space. Effective communication is key to expressing consent clearly and directly. Pay attention to non-verbal cues such as body language to understand comfort level. Consistent communication ensures that consent remains an ongoing process. Consent means continuous communication every step of the way, with a clear and enthusiastic "yes." It does not involve assumptions or pressure. Red flags indicating lack of consent include pressuring behaviors, feelings of obligation, negative reactions to refusal, and ignoring indications of non-consent. Respect in relationships involves honoring boundaries, expressing desires openly, and never assuming consent based on external factors like appearance or circumstances. Everyone has the right to their own body and should feel comfortable setting boundaries and communicating them effectively. Do not let anyone take an advantage of you. Always remember no means no.

NAVIGATING SOCIAL MEDIA SAFELY AND RESPONSIBLY

Navigating social media safely and responsibly is crucial in today's digital age to protect your online reputation and personal information. Here is a guide to help you navigate social media platforms securely. Set your social media accounts to private to control who can view your posts and interact with you. This helps in limiting access to your personal information and content. Avoid clicking on links or opening attachments from unknown sources as they may contain scams. Be cautious of unexpected messages with links, especially if they seem out of the ordinary. Refrain from sharing sensitive personal details such as your address, phone number, or financial information on social media platforms. Be mindful of what you post as once shared, it can be challenging to remove completely. Check and adjust your privacy settings on social media platforms regularly to ensure that only trusted individuals have access to your content. Stay informed about any updates in privacy policies. Be vigilant for fake profiles on social media platforms and report them promptly. Help in maintaining a secure digital environment by reporting suspicious accounts that may be engaging in fraudulent activities. Before sharing any content, consider the potential implications it may have on your reputation or privacy. Once something is posted online, it can be challenging to retract, so think carefully before posting. Set boundaries for your social media usage to prevent overexposure and potential negative effects on mental health. Familiarize yourself with the privacy features offered by each social media platform you use. Understand how these settings work and utilize them effectively to safeguard your data. If you are a parent, monitor your children's social media closely, set guidelines for usage, and educate them about online safety practices. Encourage open communication about their online experiences. By following these guidelines, you can navigate social media safely and responsibly while protecting your personal information and reputation online. Always make smart decisions!

GUIDE ON TEENAGERS DATING

Teen dating can be a significant and sometimes challenging aspect of adolescence. It's essential for both teenagers and parents to navigate this phase with care, understanding, and open communication. Teen dating today can encompass various forms, from talking and hanging out to more serious relationships. It is crucial for teenagers to be clear about their relationship status and expectations with their partner. Open communication, honesty, and mutual respect are key elements in healthy teen relationships. Parents should consider setting rules about dating before it happens to establish expectations and boundaries. Discussing these rules openly with teenagers can help align expectations and promote understanding. Rules such as age limits for dating or guidelines on physical intimacy should be explained clearly with the rationale behind them. The appropriate age for dating may vary depending on individual maturity levels rather than a specific number. Parents should focus on assessing their teenager's readiness for dating based on emotional maturity, decision-making skills, and values. Encouraging teenagers to question authority in a healthy way can lead to constructive conversations about dating rules. Parents should strive to support their teenagers in navigating relationships by being available for discussions and guidance. Encouraging open communication without judgment can help teenagers feel comfortable sharing their experiences. Providing resources such as books, articles, or counseling services can offer additional support for teens facing relationship challenges. While giving teenagers independence in their relationships is important, parents should also monitor their activities discreetly. Observing changes in behavior, mood swings, or signs of distress can indicate potential issues in the relationship that require intervention. Encouraging teens to maintain a balance between relationships, academics, extracurricular activities, and personal growth is essential. Make sure you are mature enough and ready for dating.

COMMUNICATION SKILLS

Effective communication skills are crucial for teenagers as they navigate relationships, school, and future careers. Developing good communication skills can help teenagers express themselves, build healthy relationships, and handle conflicts in a constructive manner. Helps address issues calmly and find solutions. Establishes a safe environment for open dialogue. When communicating, ensure your message is straight forward and easy to understand. Avoid using unnecessary or complex language that may confuse others. Actively listen to others by paying attention to what they are saying, maintaining eye contact, and providing verbal and non-verbal cues to show engagement. This demonstrates respect and understanding. Select the appropriate communication channel based on the nature of your message.Use face-to-face conversations for important discussions, emails for formal information, and instant messaging for quick updates. Be mindful of your tone of voice, body language, and written language as they can significantly impact how your message is received. Ensure your communication remains respectful and professional. Encourage open communication by being receptive to feedback. Constructive criticism can help you improve your communication skills and strengthen relationships with colleagues. If you are unsure about something, don't hesitate to ask questions for clarification. It is better to seek understanding than to make assumptions that could lead to misunderstandings. In a diverse workplace, respect cultural and individual differences in communication styles. Put yourself in others' shoes and try to understand their perspectives. Showing empathy can enhance trust and collaboration among team members.Use positive and constructive language when communicating with others. Positivity can create a supportive work environment and encourage teamwork. After important discussions or decisions, consider following up in writing to summarize key points. This helps ensure clarity and effective communication.

EXPLORING CAREER OPTIONS

Identify Your Interests, Values, and Skills To begin exploring career options, start by identifying what matters to you. Consider your values and skills as well. Think about what is important to you in a career beyond just salary, such as opportunities for growth, impact, or skill development and do your research. Ask yourself these questions:

- What do people in this career do on a daily basis?
- What type of work environment is typical for this career?
- What is the salary range for professionals in this field?
- Is the salary sufficient to cover your living expenses?
- Is this career projected to grow in the future?
- What education or training is required for entry into this field?

After researching different career paths, set clear goals for yourself. Determine where you see yourself in the long term and what steps you need to take to reach those goals. Commit to taking action towards exploring and pursuing your chosen career path. Career exploration is an ongoing process that may evolve over time. Regularly review your interests, values, and skills to ensure they align with your career goals. If needed, update your plan based on new information or experiences. Consider gaining practical experience through internships, part-time jobs, volunteering, or job shadowing opportunities. Practical experience can provide valuable insights into a specific industry or role and help you make informed decisions about your future career path. Don't hesitate to seek guidance from career counselors, mentors, or professionals working in fields of interest. They can provide valuable advice, insights, and networking opportunities that can further guide your exploration of different career options. Stay curious and open-minded about exploring new opportunities and industries. Continuously learn new skills, stay updated on industry trends, and be willing to adapt to changes in the job market. Embrace lifelong learning as a key aspect of navigating diverse career paths. By following these steps systematically, you can effectively explore different career options and make informed decisions about your future professional path.

FINDING THE RIGHT PATH FOR YOU

When it comes to finding the right path for yourself, especially in terms of making significant life decisions, it can be a challenging and a task. Begin by reflecting on your own values, goals, and aspirations. Consider what is truly important to you in life, both personally and professionally. Understanding your core values will provide a solid foundation for decision-making. Take the time to research different options available to you. This could involve exploring various career paths, educational opportunities, or personal choices. Gather information about each option to make an informed decision. Identify what truly excites you and where your passions lie. Choosing a path that aligns with your interests can lead to greater fulfillment and success in the long run. Assess the risks and rewards associated with each potential path. Consider both short-term and long-term implications of your decision to ensure it aligns with your overall goals. Establish clear goals for yourself and prioritize them based on their importance to you. This will help you focus on what matters most and make decisions that support your objectives. Understand that paths may change over time, and it's essential to remain flexible and adaptable as new opportunities or challenges arise. Embracing change can lead to growth and new possibilities. While it's crucial to gather information and seek advice, ultimately trust your intuition when making a decision. Listen to your gut feelings as they often provide valuable insights into what is right for you. Once you have weighed your options, made a decision based on careful consideration, take action confidently. Trust in your ability to navigate the chosen path successfully. Remember that finding the right path is a journey rather than a destination. It's okay to make mistakes along the way as they contribute to personal growth and learning experiences.

RESUME AND JOB INTERVIEW

Writing your resume should include your contact Information, include your full name, address, phone number, and email address at the top of the resume. Briefly state your career goals or summarize your skills and experiences. List your current school, expected graduation date, and any relevant coursework or achievements. Include any part-time jobs, internships, volunteer work, or extracurricular activities that demonstrate your skills. Highlight any specific skills such as computer proficiency, language abilities, or certifications. Mention any awards, honors, or accomplishments that showcase your strengths. Creating a well-crafted resume is essential when applying for your first job. Even if you don't have prior work experience, highlight your education, extracurricular activities, volunteer work, and any relevant skills or achievements. Keep your resume concise, organized, and tailored to the job you're applying for. First impressions matter, so dress appropriately when going in for an interview. Opt for business casual attire unless stated otherwise by the employer. Make sure your clothes are clean, neat, and fit well. Avoid wearing overly casual clothing like jeans and t-shirts. Before the interview, research the company you're applying to. Understand their values, mission statement, products/services, and recent news or developments. This knowledge will show your interest in the company and help you tailor your responses during the interview. Prepare for common interview questions such as, Tell me about yourself, What are your strengths and weaknesses? and Why do you want to work here? Practice your responses beforehand to feel more confident during the actual interview. During the interview, highlight relevant skills and experiences from school projects, extracurricular activities, or volunteer work that demonstrate qualities like leadership, teamwork, problem-solving, and communication skills. Provide specific examples to support your answers. At the end of the interview, be prepared to ask thoughtful questions about the role or company. This shows your interest in the position and gives you valuable insights into whether the job is a good fit for you. After the interview, send a thank-you email or note to express your gratitude for the opportunity to interview. Reiterate your interest in the position and briefly mention why you believe you're a good fit for the job.

GUIDE ON FINANCIAL LITERACY

Financial literacy empowers individuals to make informed and effective financial decisions. It encompasses various aspects of personal finance, including budgeting, saving, investing, managing debt, and understanding financial principles. Financial literacy involves the ability to comprehend and utilize a range of financial skills and concepts. This includes managing personal finances, creating budgets, investing wisely, understanding the time value of money, compound interest, debt management, and financial planning. Achieving financial literacy can lead to better decision-making and financial stability. Individuals with higher levels of financial literacy are more likely to make sound financial choices such as spending less income, creating emergency funds, and planning for retirement. In today's complex financial landscape where traditional pension plans are less common, having financial literacy is essential for retirement planning and making informed decisions about savings and investments.

Personal finance is where financial literacy translates into practical decision-making. It involves managing money effectively to achieve financial goals such as homeownership, education savings, retirement planning, and supporting family members. Key areas of personal finance include banking, budgeting, handling debt and credit, and investing. Opening a bank account is often the first step towards establishing a stable financial future. Bank accounts provide a secure place to hold money for everyday expenses and major purchases. Understanding the importance of bank accounts in safeguarding assets and facilitating financial transactions is fundamental to financial literacy. Creating a budget is essential for tracking income and expenses, identifying spending patterns, setting financial goals, and ensuring that money is allocated wisely. Budgeting helps individuals prioritize their spending, avoid overspending or accumulating debt, and work towards achieving their long-term objectives. Managing debt responsibly is a key aspect of financial literacy. Understanding different types of debt (such as student loans, credit card debt) and implementing strategies to pay off debts efficiently can help individuals maintain good credit scores and overall financial health. Investing is an important component of building wealth over time. Financially literate individuals understand investment options, risk tolerance, diversification strategies, and long-term investment goals. They make informed decisions about where to invest their money based on their individual circumstances. Learn to make good decisions concerning your money.

MANAGING YOUR MONEY

Managing money as a teenager is a crucial skill that can set the foundation for financial success later in life. By following some key principles and practices, teens can develop good money habits and secure their financial well-being. Helping teens recognize and track where they spend their money. This can be done through logging expenses in real-time, using spreadsheets, or budgeting apps. Tracking expenses helps teens understand their spending patterns, identify areas where they can save money, and promotes accountability. Teach teens to set up a budget based on their income, expenses, and financial goals. Budgeting helps differentiate between needs and wants and instills good money management practices. Utilize online budget templates or tools to categorize expenses such as clothing, entertainment, food, etc., to help teens allocate their funds effectively. Making a budget is just the first step it's essential to stick to it. Encourage teens to look for sales, make lists before shopping, and use coupons to stay within budget limits.

Instill the habit of smart shopping and avoiding unnecessary purchases to ensure the budget is followed consistently. Illustrate the power of saving by showing teens how small monthly savings can accumulate over time. Discuss concepts of interest and inflation to highlight the impact on savings. Encourage teens to set savings goals, start with small amounts, and gradually increase contributions to build long-term financial security. Educate teens on credit scores, emphasizing the importance of maintaining good credit for future financial endeavors like renting an apartment or buying a car. Teach responsible credit card usage, emphasizing timely bill payments and avoiding high balances to establish a healthy credit history. Help teens open education savings accounts or contribute to existing accounts for college savings. Encourage regular contributions from part-time job earnings or gifts received during special occasions to build a fund for higher education. Utilize resources like financial literacy tools tailored for high school students and first-year college students. Engage in courses like Financial Basics that offer practical knowledge on personal finance management and potentially lead to scholarship opportunities. Remember it's never to early to save for your retirement and never abuse your credit.

GUIDE FOR WRITING A BUSINESS PLAN FOR TEENS

Start your business plan with a concise summary of your business idea, mission statement, product or service offering, target market, and key goals. This section should provide a snapshot of your entire plan and grab the reader's attention. Provide detailed information about your company, including its history, legal structure, location, and the problem your business aims to solve. Highlight what makes your business unique and why it will be successful. Outline the products or services you will offer, their features, benefits, and how they fulfill a need in the market. Explain any competitive advantages that set your offerings apart from others. Conduct thorough research on your target market, industry trends, customer needs, and competitors. Identify opportunities and challenges in the market that could impact your business's success. Define your marketing strategy, sales approach, pricing tactics, distribution channels, and methods for reaching customers. Detail how you plan to execute your strategies effectively. Describe the organizational structure of your business, roles of team members (if applicable), and any external partners or advisors involved. Highlight the skills and experience that each team member brings to the table. Develop a comprehensive financial plan that includes startup costs, revenue projections, expenses, cash flow forecasts, break-even analysis, and potential sources of funding. Set realistic financial goals for the short-term and long-term growth of your business.

GUIDE FOR TEEN INVESTING

Investing as a teenager can be a valuable way to learn about financial responsibility and set yourself up for future success. Here is a comprehensive guide to help teens navigate the world of investing. Learn about different investment options such as stocks, bonds, mutual funds. Understand the concept of risk and return, diversification, and the power of compounding. Determine why you want to invest (e.g., saving for college, buying a car, retirement). Set specific and achievable financial goals to guide your investment decisions. Begin by investing small amounts of money that you can afford to lose. Consider using apps or platforms designed for teen investors to get started. Take advantage of online resources, books, and courses to expand your knowledge about investing. Stay informed about market trends and economic news that may impact your investments. Talk to parents, teachers, or financial advisors who can provide guidance on investing. Consider opening a custodial account with an adult to start investing under their supervision. Understand that investing is a long-term game and requires patience. Avoid making impulsive decisions based on short-term market fluctuations. Regularly review your investment portfolio and track its performance. Make adjustments as needed based on changes in your financial goals or market conditions. Embrace failures as learning opportunities in the world of investing. Analyze what went wrong and use it to make better investment decisions in the future. Develop a habit of consistently investing a portion of your income. Reinvest dividends and returns to benefit from compounding over time. Stay curious and continue learning about different investment strategies. Attend workshops, seminars, or join investment clubs to network with like-minded individuals. Following these steps and staying committed to learning and growing as an investor, teenagers can lay a solid foundation for their financial future through smart investing practices.

HEALTHY EATING HABITS FOR BUSY TEENS

In today's fast-paced world, many teens lead busy lives with school, extracurricular activities, and social engagements. Maintaining healthy eating habits can sometimes be challenging amidst a hectic schedule. However, it is crucial for teenagers to prioritize their nutrition to support their growth, development, and overall well-being. Dedicate some time each week to plan your meals. This can help you make healthier choices and avoid last-minute unhealthy options. Consider preparing meals in advance, such as on weekends or evenings when you have more time. Preparing grab-and-go options like salads, wraps, or overnight oats can save time during busy weekdays. Focus on whole foods like fruits, vegetables, whole grains, lean proteins, and healthy fats. These foods provide essential nutrients without added sugars and unhealthy fats. Keep nutritious snacks on hand such as nuts, seeds, yogurt, fruits, or cut-up veggies to curb hunger between meals. Carry a reusable water bottle with you throughout the day to stay hydrated. Avoid sugary drinks like sodas and energy drinks that provide empty calories. Incorporate protein sources like lean meats, poultry, fish, beans, lentils, tofu, or nuts in your meals to support muscle growth and repair. Start your day with a balanced breakfast that includes protein, whole grains, and fruits or vegetables to fuel your body and brain. When eating out or grabbing fast food, look for healthier options such as salads, grilled proteins, whole grain wraps or sandwiches instead of fried items or sugary beverages. Be mindful of portion sizes when dining out as restaurant servings are often larger than necessary. Pay attention to your body's hunger cues and eat when you're hungry rather than out of boredom or stress. Find alternative ways to cope with emotions instead of turning to food for comfort. Communicate with your family about your health goals so they can support you in making nutritious choices at home. If you have specific dietary concerns or need personalized guidance, consider consulting a registered dietitian for expert advice. Remember what you eat makes a difference.

THE IMPORTANCE OF EXERCISE

Regular exercise is crucial for maintaining overall health and well-being. It offers a wide range of benefits that impact various aspects of physical and mental health. Here are some key reasons why exercise is important. Exercise strengthens the heart, reduces the risk of heart disease, lowers blood pressure, and improves circulation. Regular physical activity helps in weight control by burning calories and increasing metabolism. Exercise enhances muscle strength, flexibility, and joint mobility, reducing the risk of injuries. Weight-bearing exercises help maintain bone density and reduce the risk of osteoporosis. Physical activity boosts the immune system, making the body more resilient to illnesses. Exercise releases endorphins that act as natural mood lifters, reducing stress and anxiety levels. Regular exercise improves memory, concentration, and overall cognitive function. Physical activity promotes better sleep patterns and can help alleviate insomnia. Engaging in exercise can improve self-esteem, confidence, and overall mental well-being. Regular exercise lowers the risk of chronic conditions such as diabetes, obesity, certain cancers, and cardiovascular diseases. Leading an active lifestyle is associated with a longer lifespan and improved quality of life. Exercise supports brain health by promoting neuroplasticity and reducing the risk of cognitive decline. Participating in group fitness activities or sports can foster social connections and combat feelings of isolation. Exercising with others can motivate you to achieve your fitness goals.

UNDERSTANDING PUBERTY AND BODY CHANGES

Puberty is the stage of development when children transition into young adults through physical and emotional changes. It is a gradual process that occurs over time, marked by the maturation of the reproductive system and other bodily changes. Most females begin puberty between the ages of 8 to 13, while most males start between 9 and 14. However, variations exist where some may start earlier or later than these typical ranges. Puberty is initiated by hormones released from the brain. In males, these hormones stimulate the testicles to produce testosterone and sperm. In females, they trigger the ovaries to produce estrogen and facilitate egg growth and release. Additionally, hormones from the adrenal glands contribute to secondary sexual characteristics like pubic hair growth, body odor, and acne.

Physical Changes During Puberty:

Males:

- Testicular growth
- Development of dark, coarse pubic hair
- Enlargement of penis and testes
- Increased frequency of erections
- Onset of ejaculation
- Growth of underarm and facial hair
- Voice deepening
- Gynecomastia (temporary breast growth)
- Broadening of shoulders
- Muscle development
- Growth spurt typically between ages 12 and 15

Females:

- Breast development (buds under nipples)
- Growth of pubic hair followed by underarm hair
- Widening of hips
- Weight gain and body fat increase
- Menstruation usually begins about 2 years after breast buds appear
- Growth spurt typically occurs 1–2 years before menstruation starts

GETTING ENOUGH REST IS NECESSARY

Teenagers often face challenges when it comes to getting enough rest due to various factors such as school schedules, social activities, and technology use. Here is some tips to help teenagers improve their sleep habits and ensure they get the recommended 8-10 hours of sleep per night. Encourage teens to go to bed and wake up at the same time every day, even on weekends. Consistency helps regulate the body's internal clock, making it easier to fall asleep and wake up naturally. Develop calming bedtime rituals such as reading this book, taking a warm bath, or practicing relaxation techniques. Avoid stimulating activities like using electronic devices right before bed, as the blue light can interfere with melatonin production. Ensure the bedroom is conducive to sleep by keeping it dark, quiet, and cool. Invest in comfortable bedding and pillows to promote better sleep quality. Encourage teens to power down electronic devices at least an hour before bedtime. The exposure to screens can disrupt sleep patterns and make it harder to fall asleep. Discourage the consumption of caffeinated beverages or large meals close to bedtime. Regular physical activity can promote better sleep quality. Encourage teens to engage in exercise earlier in the day rather than close to bedtime. If a teenager consistently struggles with sleep despite following good sleep hygiene practices, consider consulting a healthcare professional. Addressing underlying sleep disorders or issues can significantly improve overall restfulness. Don't forget to turn off the lights and get a good night sleep!

HOW TO NAVIGATE THE TEENAGE YEARS

The teenage years are a time of significant change and growth. Navigating this period can be challenging, but with the right guidance, you can make the most out of these transformative years. Here's a comprehensive guide to help you through your teenage journey. This period involves numerous physical, emotional, and social changes. Even though you may prefer hanging out with friends, spending time with family is important. Participate in family meals or activities. Make an effort to spend alone time with your parents or guardians. This could be during car rides, at a favorite restaurant, or while engaging in a shared hobby. Set aside distraction-free time to talk with your parents or guardians. Listen actively and share your thoughts openly. It's okay to disagree with your parents but do so respectfully. Express your feelings without dismissing theirs. Learn to negotiate and compromise on conflicts. Offer solutions and be willing to listen to their perspective. Focus on discussing behaviors rather than attitudes when resolving conflicts. Use this time to explore different aspects of your identity through clothes, hairstyles, music, etc. Be aware of the content you consume in music, movies, and video games.Take on responsibilities like holding a job or helping with household chores. Make decisions independently but seek guidance when needed. Ensure you attend annual health check-ups to monitor physical changes. Pay attention to your mental health by talking about your feelings and seeking support when necessary. Understand that mistakes are part of growing up. Seek advice from trusted adults like teachers or doctors if you're facing difficulties. Develop the confidence to say no when faced with peer pressure that goes against your values or safety. Engage in activities that build skills such as teamwork, leadership, and problem-solving. Believe in yourself and express confidence in your ability to grow into a responsible adult.

HOW TO AVOID GETTING SICK

To avoid getting sick, especially for teenagers who are more susceptible to colds and other illnesses, here are some essential tips. Practice regular handwashing with soap and water, especially before eating, after using the restroom, and after being in public places. Proper hand hygiene can significantly reduce the spread of germs. Eating a balanced diet rich in fruits and vegetables, staying hydrated by drinking plenty of water, getting regular exercise, and ensuring an adequate amount of sleep can help boost the immune system and overall health. Try to stay away from people who are sick to minimize exposure to viruses and bacteria that can cause illnesses like colds. Regularly disinfect commonly touched surfaces such as doorknobs, light switches, and electronic devices to reduce the spread of germs. High levels of stress can weaken the immune system, making it easier to get sick. Practice stress-reducing activities such as exercise, meditation, or hobbies you enjoy. Refrain from sharing items like utensils, water bottles, or makeup with others to prevent the spread of germs. If you do feel unwell, it's essential to stay home from school or social activities to prevent spreading illness to others and give your body time to rest and recover. Cover your mouth and nose with a tissue or your elbow when coughing or sneezing to prevent the spread of respiratory droplets that can contain viruses. Consider incorporating immune-boosting foods like citrus fruits, yogurt with probiotics, garlic, ginger, and green tea into your diet to support your body's defenses against infections. Don't forget to wash your hands often!

HYGIENE IS IMPORTANT

Teenagers go through significant physical and hormonal changes during adolescence, making personal hygiene crucial for their health, confidence, and social interactions. Here is a comprehensive guide on hygiene for teenagers to help them navigate this important aspect of self-care. Daily showering becomes essential during puberty to maintain cleanliness and prevent body odor. Use a mild soap and focus on washing the face, hands, feet, underarms, groin, bottom, and under the fingernails. Discuss the frequency of hair washing with your teen based on their hair type. Some teens may choose to wash their hair daily to manage oiliness or skip days to prevent dryness. With increased sweat gland activity during puberty, using deodorant or antiperspirant daily becomes important. Help your teen understand the difference between deodorants that mask odor and antiperspirants that control sweating. Emphasize the importance of wearing clean clothes daily after puberty hits. Cotton clothing can help absorb sweat better than synthetic materials. Encourage your teen to wash their face twice a day to prevent acne. Caution against over-washing or scrubbing vigorously as it can lead to skin irritation. Stress the significance of brushing teeth twice a day and flossing regularly to maintain oral health. Schedule regular dental check-ups for your teenager to prevent issues like bad breath and tooth decay. Remind your teen to pay attention to foot hygiene by washing thoroughly in the shower and ensuring feet are completely dry before putting on shoes. Encourage wearing cotton socks and alternating shoes to prevent smelly feet. Teach your teen about keeping their genitals clean with gentle washing using warm water and mild soap. Emphasize avoiding cleaning products or perfumes inside sensitive areas. Guide your daughter on managing periods with pads, tampons, menstrual cups, or period-proof underwear. Introduce shaving practices when facial hair starts growing and teach proper techniques using razors and shaving cream. Remember your hygiene is important to you and your health.

WHAT GIRLS CAN EXPECT DURING THEIR MENSTRUAL CYCLE

During their menstrual cycle, teenage girls can expect a variety of physical and emotional changes. The main feature of a period is the release of blood from the uterus through the vagina. This bleeding typically lasts around 5 days but can vary. Many girls experience abdominal cramps during their period, which can range from mild to severe. These cramps are caused by the contractions of the uterus as it sheds its lining. Hormonal fluctuations during the menstrual cycle can lead to mood changes such as irritability, sadness, or anxiety. Some girls may experience bloating, which is often due to water retention associated with hormonal changes. Hormonal changes can also contribute to breakouts or worsening of acne during the menstrual cycle. The breasts may feel tender or swollen due to hormonal shifts. Girls will need to use menstrual hygiene products like pads, tampons, or menstrual cups to manage the flow of blood during their period. It's essential for girls to change their pads, tampons, or cups regularly (about every 3-6 hours) to maintain hygiene and prevent leaks. Initially, after getting their first period (menarche), teenage girls may experience irregular cycles where the timing and symptoms vary. Over time, most girls cycles become more regular, occurring approximately once every 4-5 weeks. Some girls may experience premenstrual symptoms such as moodiness, bloating, and acne in the days leading up to their period. These symptoms usually resolve within a few days after menstruation begins. Around midway through the menstrual cycle (typically about two weeks before the next period), ovulation occurs when an egg is released from the ovary. Some girls may experience mild discomfort or spotting during ovulation. Puberty-related changes like breast development, growth of pubic hair, and body shape alterations often precede a girl's first period.

HOW TO MANAGE STRESS EFFECTIVELY

Managing stress effectively as a teenager is crucial for maintaining overall well-being and mental health. Here is a comprehensive guide with practical tips to help teenagers navigate and cope with stress. Recognize the sources of stress in your life, such as school pressure, social relationships, family issues, or personal expectations. Understanding what triggers your stress is the first step in managing it effectively. Eat nutritious foods that fuel your body and mind. Avoid excessive caffeine, sugar, and processed foods that can contribute to mood swings and energy crashes. Engage in physical activities you enjoy, whether it's sports, dancing, yoga, or simply going for a walk. Exercise helps reduce stress hormones and promotes overall well-being. Prioritize getting enough sleep each night to allow your body and mind to rest and recharge. Establish a bedtime routine and limit screen time before bed for better sleep quality. Use a planner or digital calendar to organize your daily tasks, assignments, extracurricular activities, and personal time. Setting aside dedicated time for studying, relaxation, and hobbies can help reduce feelings of being overwhelmed. Incorporate deep breathing exercises into your daily routine to calm your mind and body during stressful moments. Learn mindfulness techniques to stay present in the moment and manage racing thoughts or anxiety. Don't hesitate to reach out to trusted friends, family members, teachers, or counselors when you need someone to listen. If stress becomes overwhelming or affects your daily life significantly, consider seeking support from a mental health professional for therapy or counseling. Dedicate time to activities you enjoy, whether it's painting, playing music, reading, or spending time outdoors. Maintain healthy relationships with friends who uplift you and provide emotional support during challenging times. Learn to say no to additional commitments that may increase your stress levels unnecessarily. Allow yourself breaks throughout the day to relax and recharge.

DEALING WITH PEER PRESSURE

Peer pressure is a common experience for many individuals, especially during adolescence and young adulthood. It can manifest in various forms, both positive and negative, influencing behaviors, decisions, and self-perception. Handling peer pressure effectively requires awareness, confidence, and the ability to make independent choices aligned with personal values. Recognize the different types of peer pressure, including positive influences that encourage growth and negative influences that may lead to risky or harmful behaviors. Acknowledge that peer pressure is a normal part of social interactions but should not compromise your values or well-being. Pay attention to your feelings and intuition in social situations. If something doesn't feel right or align with your beliefs, it's essential to trust yourself and your judgment. Remember that it's okay to say no and prioritize your own well-being over fitting in with a group. Define your values, boundaries, and limits before hand to have a clear understanding of what you are comfortable with and what crosses the line for you. Communicate your boundaries assertively but respectfully when faced with peer pressure situations. Cultivate friendships with individuals who respect your choices, values, and individuality. Seek out like-minded peers who share similar beliefs and can provide encouragement in resisting negative peer influences. Practice assertive communication techniques to express your thoughts, feelings, and decisions confidently without feeling pressured to conform. Learn how to say no firmly yet politely when faced with unwanted peer pressure. Confide in parents, teachers, mentors, or counselors about challenging peer pressure situations you encounter. Utilize the support and guidance of trusted adults to navigate difficult social dynamics and make informed decisions. Focus on developing a strong sense of self-worth and confidence in your identity independent of external influences. Engage in activities that boost self-awareness, self-care practices, and positive self-image. Be a role model for positive behavior by encouraging kindness, empathy, inclusivity, and ethical decision-making among peers. Foster a supportive environment where individuals feel empowered to make healthy choices without fear of judgment or rejection.

HOW TEENAGERS CAN DEAL WITH CYBERBULLYING

Teenagers facing cyberbullying can take several steps to address and cope with the situation effectively. Teenagers should remain calm and step away from the device or computer if they encounter cyberbullying. Taking a break can help them avoid immediate emotional reactions. Teenagers should ignore hurtful messages or posts from bullies and block them on social media platforms or messaging apps. Blocking the bully can prevent further negative interactions. In cases where cyberbullying persists, teenagers should save and document any bullying messages, images, or videos as evidence. This documentation may be necessary when reporting the bullying. Teenagers should confide in a trusted adult, such as a parent, teacher, school counselor, or another responsible individual. Talking about their experiences can provide emotional support. Teens should report instances of cyberbullying to relevant platforms or authorities. Social media sites often have mechanisms for reporting abusive behavior, and mobile phone providers can assist in blocking harassing numbers. Encourage teenagers to reach out to friends for support. Peer support can be crucial in combating cyberbullying and creating a network of allies against bullies. Developing empathy and awareness of these roles can empower teens to navigate online interactions more effectively. Educate teenagers about online safety practices, such as setting privacy controls on social media accounts, being cautious about sharing personal information online, and avoiding engaging with unknown individuals. Teens if you are being bullying please report it to your trusted adult or local police.

BASIC COOKING SKILLS EVERY TEEN SHOULD LEARN

Teens should learn how to budget, plan a menu, and shop for groceries efficiently. They need to understand the importance of fresh produce, meal planning, sticking to a budget. Teaching teens how to handle knives safely and effectively is crucial. They should learn basic cutting techniques, knife handling, and the purpose of different types of knives in the kitchen. It's essential for teens to be aware of kitchen safety practices, including how to prevent accidents, handle burns or cuts, and know basic first aid procedures related to cooking mishaps. Understanding how to operate common kitchen appliances like stoves, ovens, microwaves, blenders, and slow cookers is important for teens. They should also learn about safety precautions when using these appliances. Teens need to grasp the concept of accurate measuring and weighing of ingredients for recipes. This includes using measuring cups and spoons correctly for both dry and liquid ingredients, as well as understanding when weight measurements are necessary. Learning how to read recipes thoroughly, follow instructions step by step, and clarify any uncertainties before starting the cooking process is a fundamental skill for teens in the kitchen. Being able to adjust recipe quantities by cutting them down for smaller servings or doubling them for larger groups is a valuable skill that helps teens prepare recipes according to their needs. Teaching teens the importance of having all ingredients prepared and ready before cooking instills good habits that lead to organized and efficient cooking sessions. If you master these basic cooking skills, teens can develop confidence in the kitchen, create delicious meals independently, and cultivate a lifelong appreciation for cooking and healthy eating habits.

CREATING YOUR OWN SPACE

Teenagers can create their own space by personalizing their bedroom. They can choose their own decorations, colors, and furniture to reflect their style and preferences. This allows them to have a space that feels uniquely theirs and where they can express themselves. Another way for teenagers to create their own space is by setting up a study or creative corner in the house. This area can be designated for activities such as studying, reading, drawing, or pursuing hobbies. Having a dedicated space for these activities can help teenagers focus and feel more comfortable. Teenagers can also create their own space outdoors, if available. This could involve setting up a cozy corner in the garden, creating a hangout spot on the patio, or even having a small shed or studio where they can spend time alone or with friends. Outdoor spaces provide a change of scenery and fresh air, which can be beneficial for relaxation and creativity. To truly make their space their own, teenagers should communicate with family members about boundaries and expectations regarding privacy and respect for their personal area. Setting clear guidelines on when the space is off-limits to others can help teenagers feel like they have control over their environment. Encouraging teenagers to organize and declutter their space can also help them create a more functional and enjoyable environment. By getting rid of unnecessary items and keeping things tidy, they can make the most of the space they have and feel more at ease in it. Adding personal touches such as photos, artwork, posters, or mementos can further enhance the sense of ownership over their space. These items can make the area feel cozy and reflective of their interests and memories. While teenagers should create their own space, seeking input from parents or guardians can also be valuable. Collaborating on design ideas or discussing practical considerations can lead to a space that meets both the teenager's needs and the family's expectations.

HOW TO KEEP THE ENVIRONMENT SAFE AND CLEAN

To keep the environment safe and clean there are several actions that can be taken on a daily basis to contribute to environmental conservation and sustainability. Here are some steps that teenagers can follow. Take shorter showers to conserve water, be mindful while brushing teeth or washing hands, fix any leaks in faucets or pipes promptly, use a bucket instead of running water when cleaning vehicles. Turn off lights and unplug electronic devices when not in use, open windows for natural light and ventilation instead of using artificial lighting and air conditioning. Separate recyclable materials like paper, plastic, glass, and metal for recycling. Avoid single-use plastics by using reusable alternatives like water bottles and bags. Donate or sell items you no longer need instead of throwing them away. Walk, bike, or use public transportation whenever possible to reduce carbon emissions from vehicles. Carpool with friends or family members to minimize the number of cars on the road. Purchase products made from sustainable materials that are biodegradable or recyclable. Join local environmental organizations or volunteer for community clean-up events. Participate in awareness campaigns about environmental issues at school or in your community.

HEAL FROM THE DEATH OF A LOVED ONE

Teenagers who are grieving the death of a loved one can benefit greatly from seeking support from trusted individuals such as family members, friends, or adult mentors. It is essential for teenagers to have a support system in place that they can rely on during this difficult time. Grief counselors, therapists, and support groups can also provide valuable assistance in navigating the grieving process. Encouraging teenagers to express their emotions and thoughts can be crucial in helping them heal from the loss of a loved one. Some teenagers may find solace in talking about their feelings, while others may prefer alternative methods of expression such as writing in a journal, creating art, or engaging in other creative activities. Providing teenagers with various outlets to express themselves can aid in processing their grief. Creating opportunities for teenagers to preserve memories of the deceased loved one can be a meaningful way to cope with grief. Encouraging them to engage in activities that honor the memory of their loved one, such as planting a tree, participating in charitable events, or creating a memory box, can help keep the connection alive. Writing letters or gratitude notes to the deceased can also be a therapeutic way for teenagers to express their feelings and maintain a sense of closeness. Involving teenagers in rituals such as memorial services or funerals provides them with an opportunity to gather with others who knew their loved one and share in the collective mourning process. These gatherings can offer comfort and support as teenagers navigate their grief journey alongside friends and family members who understand their loss. It is important for teenagers to recognize that healing from the death of a loved one is a gradual process that takes time. They should allow themselves the space and patience needed to grieve at their own pace without feeling pressured to "move on" before they are ready. Understanding that healing does not mean forgetting the person who died but rather finding ways to carry their memory forward can help teenagers cope with their loss.

MENDING A BROKEN HEART

It is essential for teenagers to avoid contact with their ex-partner, especially when they are feeling sensitive after a breakup. Trying to maintain a friendship immediately after a breakup may not be beneficial. Encourage teenagers to talk about their feelings with friends or family members they trust. Expressing emotions and sharing experiences can help in processing the breakup and gaining support from loved ones. Allowing oneself to cry and feel the emotions associated with the breakup is important for healing. Holding back tears can prolong the pain, so it's healthy to let the tears flow as a way of releasing sorrow. It's crucial for teenagers to understand that trying to get back together with an ex out of loneliness or sadness is not a good idea. Rekindling the relationship without addressing underlying issues can lead to further heartache. Keeping reminders of the ex-partner, such as gifts or photos, can intensify feelings of sadness and longing. It's advisable for teenagers to remove these reminders from sight to aid in moving on from the relationship. Healing from a broken heart takes time, and it's important for teenagers to be patient with themselves during this process. Time is a significant factor in gradually overcoming the pain of a breakup.

TEENAGERS RESPONSIBILITY TOWARDS ADULTS

In the journey towards increased independence and young adulthood, teenagers have a significant responsibility towards adults. This responsibility encompasses various aspects that contribute to their personal growth and development as responsible adults. One crucial aspect of teenagers' responsibility towards adults is showing respect and maintaining open communication. Respect for adults, including parents, teachers, and other authority figures, is essential in fostering positive relationships and demonstrating maturity. Teenagers should communicate openly and honestly with adults, expressing their thoughts and feelings in a respectful manner. Teenagers have a responsibility to follow rules and guidelines set by adults, whether at home, school, or in the community. Adhering to curfews, household rules, school policies, and societal norms demonstrates accountability and respect for authority. By obeying rules, teenagers show that they understand the importance of structure and boundaries in their lives. Another aspect of teenagers' responsibility towards adults is contributing positively to the community. This can involve volunteering, participating in community service projects, or engaging in activities that benefit others. By giving back to the community, teenagers learn the value of altruism, empathy, and social responsibility under the guidance of adults. Teenagers also have a responsibility to seek guidance and support from adults when needed. Whether facing challenges at school, dealing with peer pressure, or making important decisions about their future, teenagers should feel comfortable turning to trusted adults for advice and assistance. Seeking mentorship from adults can help teenagers navigate complex situations and make informed choices. As emerging young adults, teenagers bear the responsibility of setting a positive example for younger children and peers. By demonstrating integrity, kindness, resilience, and ethical behavior in their interactions with others, teenagers inspire those around them to emulate positive traits. Serving as role models within their communities reflects teenagers' commitment to upholding values upheld by adults.

DRIVING SAFETY TIPS FOR NEW DRIVERS

Driving can be an exciting and liberating experience, especially for new drivers who have recently obtained their driver's license. However, it is crucial to prioritize safety on the road to protect yourself and others. Here are some essential driving safety tips for new drivers. Before hitting the road, familiarize yourself with the vehicle you will be driving. Understand the location of all controls, such as signal lights, headlights, windshield wipers, and emergency flashers. Make sure all lights are working correctly, especially if you plan to drive at night. Adhering to traffic rules is fundamental for safe driving. Follow speed limits, yield right-of-way when required, obey traffic signals, and always wear your seatbelt. Understanding and applying traffic regulations not only keep you safe but also contribute to a relaxed driving experience for everyone on the road. Regular maintenance is essential to ensure your vehicle operates smoothly and safely. Schedule routine oil changes, check tire pressure regularly (including the spare tire), rotate tires as recommended, monitor brake fluid and coolant levels, and keep your gas tank filled. Proper vehicle maintenance reduces the risk of breakdowns and potential accidents. Distracted driving is a leading cause of accidents on the road. Stay focused by refraining from texting, calling, eating, or engaging in other distracting activities while driving. Set up your music playlist, GPS navigation, and phone settings before starting your journey to minimize distractions. Ensure your seat position is comfortable and adjust all mirrors to eliminate blind spots. Before driving off, confirm that objects passing behind you appear in the side mirrors as they disappear from the rearview mirror. Properly adjusting accessories enhances visibility and overall safety while driving. Avoid tailgating by adhering to the three-second rule—select an object on the road ahead and ensure you maintain a three-second gap between your vehicle and the one in front of you. Keeping a safe following distance reduces the risk of rear-end collisions. Equip your vehicle with essential documents such as registration, insurance proof, and driver's license at all times. Additionally, carry an emergency kit containing items like water, non-perishable snacks, blankets, flashlights, road hazard cones or flares, jumper cables, basic tools, oil, and coolant. Stay vigilant of changing weather conditions such as rain or snow that can impact driving safety. Adjust your driving behavior by turning on headlights in low visibility conditions, reducing speed on slick roads, and increasing following distance to allow for longer braking distances. Always remember safety first!

WHAT YOU NEED TO KNOW ABOUT CREDIT

Building credit is an essential financial skill for teenagers as it sets the foundation for their future financial stability. Here are key points that teenagers should know about credit. A credit score is a three-digit number that indicates how likely an individual is to repay borrowed money. The score ranges from 300 to 850, with different categories such as excellent, very good, good, fair, and poor credit. Factors that determine a credit score include payment history, amounts owed, length of credit history, types of credit in use, and account inquiries. Credit scores impact eligibility for loans, interest rates on loans and credit cards, renting apartments, utility payments, and even job prospects. Maintaining a good credit score can lead to lower interest rates and easier access to financial resources in the future. Becoming an authorized user on someone's credit card can help establish credit for teens. Applying for a credit card when eligible and using it responsibly can also build credit over time. Paying bills on time and keeping debt levels low are crucial steps in building a positive credit history. Monitoring your credit report regularly helps identify any errors or fraudulent activity. Free copies of credit reports can be obtained annually. A credit report provides a summary of an individual's financial habits, including payment history and debt obligations. Developing a positive credit history early on can lead to better financial opportunities later in life.

GUIDE FOR APPLYING FOR GRANTS FOR COLLEGES

When it comes to applying for grants for college, there are several key steps that teens can follow to increase their chances of securing financial aid. Here is a comprehensive guide for teens looking to apply for grants. Public Student Grants, these grants come from public funds and are typically need-based. Teens should be aware of federal grants like the Pell Grant and state-specific grants. Federal grants, such as the Pell Grant, are provided by the U.S. Department of Education. Understanding eligibility criteria and application processes for federal grants is crucial. Merit-Based Grants are awarded based on merit, so teens should focus on showcasing their academic performance, extracurricular activities, and leadership roles. Formula grants are need-based and require submission of the Free Application for Federal Student Aid (FAFSA). Teens should ensure they complete the FAFSA accurately. Teens should research different grant opportunities available at the federal, state, and institutional levels.

They can explore websites like Grants.gov and their state's higher education agency website for information on available grants. Teens should gather all required documents, including tax information, academic transcripts, letters of recommendation, and any other supporting materials needed for grant applications. It is essential for teens to submit their grant applications early to meet deadlines and maximize their chances of receiving funding. Late applications may not be considered. Teens can seek guidance from school counselors, financial aid offices, or online resources to navigate the grant application process effectively.

REASONS YOU SHOULD NOT PURCHASE OR PLAY WITH GUNS

Teenagers should not purchase or play with guns due to several critical reasons. Teenagers may lack the maturity and experience to handle firearms safely, leading to a higher risk of accidents, injuries, or fatalities. Inexperience and impulsivity can result in mishandling guns, accidental discharges, or improper storage practices. In many jurisdictions, it is illegal for individuals under a certain age to purchase or possess firearms. Teenagers who acquire guns illegally may face severe legal consequences, including criminal charges and imprisonment. Engaging in unlawful activities related to firearms can have long-lasting repercussions on their future. Adolescence is a period of significant emotional and psychological development. Introducing guns into this vulnerable stage of life can have detrimental effects on mental health and decision-making abilities. Access to firearms may increase the likelihood of impulsive actions during moments of emotional distress. Teenagers are susceptible to peer pressure and influence from their social circles. Owning or playing with guns as a result of peer influence can lead to dangerous situations, such as showing off firearms irresponsibly or engaging in risky behaviors for acceptance among peers. Research indicates that the presence of firearms in households with teenagers increases the risk of violence, including self-harm, suicide attempts, accidental shootings, or involvement in violent altercations. Easy access to guns can escalate conflicts and endanger both the teenager and those around them. Teenagers may not have received adequate training in firearm safety and responsible gun handling practices. Without proper education on how to use, store, and secure firearms correctly, teenagers are more likely to commit errors that could result in tragic outcomes. Parents or guardians play a crucial role in ensuring the safety of teenagers regarding firearms. Allowing teenagers unrestricted access to guns without supervision or guidance neglects parental responsibility for safeguarding their children from harm. Due to the combination of physical risks, legal implications, developmental considerations, social influences, potential for violence, lack of training, and parental responsibilities involved, it is highly advisable that teenagers do not purchase or play with guns.

REASONS YOU SHOULD NOT DO DRUGS, ALCOHOL, OR JOIN GANGS

Teenagers should avoid drugs, alcohol, and gang involvement due to the significant negative consequences associated with these behaviors. Here are the reasons why teenagers should steer clear of these activities. Drugs and Alcohol, substance abuse can have severe health implications, including addiction, overdose, organ damage, mental health disorders, impaired cognitive function, and increased risk of accidents or injuries. Gang activities often involve violence, which can lead to physical harm, injuries, or even death. Additionally, gang members may be exposed to substance abuse within the gang culture. Underage drinking and drug use are illegal and can result in legal repercussions such as fines, community service, suspension of driver's license, or even criminal charges. Participation in gang-related criminal activities can lead to arrests, imprisonment, and a permanent criminal record that can severely impact future opportunities. Substance abuse can strain relationships with family and friends, lead to social isolation, and contribute to mental health issues such as depression and anxiety. Joining a gang can alienate teenagers from positive social circles, expose them to dangerous situations that threaten their safety and well-being, and perpetuate a cycle of violence. Substance abuse can impair academic performance, leading to truancy, dropout rates, decreased educational attainment, and limited future opportunities. Gang activities often interfere with school attendance and engagement in learning activities due to the demands of gang involvement. Substance abuse can hinder teenagers' ability to pursue higher education or secure employment due to its negative impact on physical health, mental well-being, and overall productivity. Being associated with gangs can limit future prospects by stigmatizing individuals in the eyes of society and potential employers. Value your life and future.

WHAT TO EXPECT AFTER HIGH SCHOOL AND CHOICES TO CONSIDER

Graduating from high school is a significant milestone that opens up a world of possibilities. As you transition into this new phase of life, it's essential to understand what to expect and the various choices available to you. Here's a comprehensive overview. The period after high school can be both exciting and daunting. You may experience a mix of emotions, including freedom, anxiety, and uncertainty about the future. It's normal to feel overwhelmed by the multitude of options available, and it's important to give yourself time to adjust. One of the most common routes after high school is to further your education. Here are several educational options you might consider. Pursuing a bachelor's degree can provide specialized knowledge in your field of interest. Researching schools, courses, and scholarship opportunities is crucial. This option offers a more affordable way to earn an associate degree or complete general education requirements before transferring to a four-year institution. If you prefer hands-on work, trade schools offer practical training in specific trades like plumbing, electrical work, or culinary arts. Short-term programs that focus on specific skills can help you enter the workforce quickly in fields like IT or healthcare. These intensive programs teach technical skills in areas such as coding or digital marketing over a short period. With numerous online resources available, you can learn valuable skills independently without formal education. If immediate employment appeals to you, there are many job opportunities that don't require a college degree. Gaining experience through internships allows you to learn while earning money. Positions in sales, hospitality, retail, and customer service often require only a high school diploma. Flexible jobs like driving for rideshare services or delivering food can provide income while allowing time for exploration. Consider taking time off for personal growth through experiences such as traveling or volunteering during a gap year can provide valuable life experiences and help clarify your future goals. Exploring new places broadens your perspective and helps you discover what interests you. Engaging in community service not only benefits others but also enhances your resume and personal development. Regardless of the path you choose, developing essential skills will benefit your future endeavors. Focus on acquiring career-specific skills relevant to your chosen field. Communication, teamwork, problem-solving, and leadership abilities are crucial in any job setting. Learning how to manage finances, cook healthy meals, and navigate daily responsibilities will serve you well as an adult. If you're unsure about what direction to take after high school. Reflect on what excites you and explore all options while considering your interests and goals.

WHAT TO DO WHEN YOU ARE PULLED OVER BY A POLICE OFFICER

When you are pulled over by a police officer, it is essential to remain calm and follow specific steps to ensure your safety and the safety of the officer. Here's a comprehensive guide on what to do. As soon as you see the police lights behind you, take a deep breath to stay calm. Activate your turn signal to indicate that you intend to pull over. Find a safe place to pull over, ideally as far to the right side of the road as possible. If you are on a busy road or highway, look for a well-lit area if it is nighttime. Once stopped, turn off your vehicle's engine. Silence any music or audio devices to minimize distractions. Place your hands on the steering wheel where they are easily visible to the officer. If you have passengers, instruct them to keep their hands visible as well. Remain in your vehicle unless instructed otherwise by the officer. Do not make sudden movements; wait for the officer to approach. When the officer approaches, lower your window for better communication. If you have any weapons in the vehicle, inform the officer about their presence immediately. When asked, provide your driver's license, registration, and proof of insurance. If these documents are out of reach (e.g., in your glove compartment), inform the officer where they are before reaching for them. Listen attentively and follow all instructions given by the officer. If you have questions or need clarification about what is happening, ask respectfully. Understand your rights. You have the right to remain silent; you do not have to answer questions beyond identifying yourself. You can refuse consent for searches but be aware that officers may still conduct searches under certain circumstances. After receiving any citations or warnings, merge back into traffic cautiously once it is safe. Remember that signing a ticket is not an admission of guilt; it simply acknowledges receipt of the citation. If you following these steps during a traffic stop, you can help ensure that both you and the police officer remain safe throughout the encounter.

SENSES ON A SPIRITUAL LEVEL

To exercise your senses on a spiritual level according to God's word, teenagers can engage in various practices that help them connect with their spirituality and deepen their relationship with God. Here are some ways teenagers can exercise their senses spiritually based on biblical principles. Prayer is a powerful tool for communication with God. Encouraging teenagers to establish a regular prayer routine can help them develop a deeper connection with the divine. Through prayer, teenagers can express gratitude, seek guidance, and cultivate a sense of peace and inner strength. Meditation, on the other hand, allows individuals to quiet their minds, focus on God's presence, and listen for His voice. By incorporating both prayer and meditation into their daily lives, teenagers can enhance their spiritual awareness and sensitivity. The Bible is considered the ultimate source of spiritual wisdom and guidance for Christians. Encouraging teenagers to study scripture regularly can help them gain insights into God's teachings, principles, and promises. By immersing themselves in the word of God, teenagers can sharpen their spiritual discernment, deepen their understanding of God's will, and strengthen their faith. Group Bible studies or devotional readings can also provide opportunities for teenagers to discuss and reflect on biblical truths together. Participating in worship services and fellowship activities with other believers can be a transformative experience for teenagers seeking to exercise their senses spiritually. Worshiping God through music, prayer, and praise can evoke powerful emotions and create a sense of unity within the community of faith. Fellowship with like-minded peers allows teenagers to share experiences, support one another in their spiritual journey, and build lasting relationships based on mutual faith and values. According to biblical teachings, serving others is an essential aspect of living out one's faith. Encouraging teenagers to engage in acts of service and compassion towards those in need can help them cultivate empathy, humility, and love for others. By volunteering at local charities, participating in mission trips, or simply helping out within their communities, teenagers can put their faith into action and experience the joy of making a positive impact in the world. Gratitude is a virtue that is highly valued in many religious traditions, including Christianity. Teaching teenagers to cultivate a spirit of thankfulness towards God for His blessings and provisions can help them develop a more positive outlook on life and nurture a sense of contentment regardless of circumstances. Encouraging them to keep gratitude journals or regularly express appreciation for the people around them can foster an attitude of humility and appreciation for the goodness of God.

WHAT THE BIBLE SAY TO CHILDREN

In the Bible, there are several verses that provide guidance and wisdom specifically directed towards children. These verses emphasize the importance of obedience, respect, and faith in God among children. Here are some key Bible verses that address children directly:

1. **Colossians 3:20**: "Children, obey your parents in everything, for this pleases the Lord."
2. **Proverbs 20:11**: "Even a child makes himself known by his acts, by whether his conduct is pure and upright."
3. **Proverbs 1:8-9**: "Hear, my son, your father's instruction, and forsake not your mother's teaching, for they are a graceful garland for your head and pendants for your neck."

4. **Matthew 19:14**: "Jesus said, 'Let the little children come to me, and do not hinder them, for the kingdom of heaven belongs to such as these.'"
5. **Proverbs 22:6**: "Train up a child in the way he should go; even when he is old he will not depart from it."

These verses highlight the importance of obedience to parents, displaying good behavior as a reflection of one's character, listening to parental teachings with respect, and ultimately coming to Jesus with childlike faith.

SPIRITUAL GUIDANCE

Spirituality is a deeply personal journey that can provide numerous benefits to teens, including higher self-esteem, positive relationships, a sense of purpose, and reduced stress and anxiety. Here is a comprehensive guide to help teens explore and develop their spiritual practice. Understanding that spirituality is about connecting to something greater than oneself, whether it's a deity, nature, or a set of beliefs that inspire wonder and humility. Recognize that spirituality is distinct from organized religion and can be personalized based on individual beliefs and experiences. Engaging in spiritual practices can boost self-worth and confidence. Spirituality can foster healthier connections with others. Teens may find meaning and direction in life through spiritual exploration. Feeling connected to something greater can provide a sense of belonging. Spiritual practices often help reduce anxiety and stress levels. Encourage teens to explore different forms of prayer, whether traditional or spontaneous.

Introduce various meditation techniques like silent contemplation, breathing exercises, or mantra meditation. Encourage reading sacred texts or listening to spiritual teachings for inspiration. Spending time in nature can be a powerful way to connect spiritually. Engaging in creative activities like art, music, or writing can also be a form of spiritual practice. Encourage teens to reflect on what brings them joy, peace, and a sense of connection. Allow space for experimentation with different spiritual practices to find what resonates best. Emphasize the importance of regular practice to deepen spiritual connections over time. By exploring these aspects of spirituality and incorporating them into their lives, teens can cultivate a deeper sense of self-awareness, resilience, and inner peace.

ENCOURAGING AND EMPOWERING TEENS WORLDWIDE

To all teenagers worldwide, it is essential to recognize the potential impact Teens can have on society. Here are some key ways to empower and support teenagers globally. Encourage teens to develop a personal relationship with God and understand the core beliefs of Christianity. Promote regular prayer and Bible reading among teens, emphasizing the importance of spiritual practices. Provide opportunities for teens to engage in discussions about faith and share their beliefs with others. Offer support and resources for teens dealing with mental health issues such as depression and suicidal thoughts. Open up conversations about sensitive topics like pornography and sexual activity, providing guidance and education on healthy relationships. Advocate for a holistic approach to mental health that includes spiritual well-being alongside medical interventions. Educate teens about the potential negative impacts of excessive social media use on mental health. Encourage responsible online behavior and promote digital well-being practices among teenagers. Emphasize the importance of real-life connections and activities beyond the digital realm. To all teens all over the world remember you are unique in your own ways and embrace your uniqueness. Practice making good chioces now will lead you to a brighter future.

BE PREPARED AND ARMOR YOURSELF

The Armor of God is a metaphorical representation of the spiritual protection that Christians should put on daily to stand against the schemes of the devil, as described by the bible in Ephesians 6:10-18. Here is a guide on how teenagers can understand and apply each piece of the armor. The belt of truth represents living a life based on honesty and integrity, grounded in the truth of God's Word. Encourage teenagers to always speak the truth, avoid deception, and seek wisdom from the Bible to guide their decisions. The breastplate protects the heart and vital organs, symbolizing righteousness and moral purity. Teach teenagers to make choices that align with God's standards, avoiding actions or behaviors that compromise their integrity. Just as shoes provide stability and mobility, the shoes of peace represent readiness to share the message of peace found in the Gospel. Encourage teenagers to be peacemakers, share their faith with others, and live out the teachings of Jesus in their daily interactions. The shield is used to block attacks from the enemy, symbolizing faith as a defense against doubts and temptations. Help teenagers strengthen their faith through prayer, reading Scripture, and surrounding themselves with supportive Christian community. The helmet protects the mind and thoughts, representing salvation through Christ and assurance of eternal life. Guide teenagers to understand their identity in Christ, reminding them of God's love and grace in moments of doubt or insecurity. The sword represents the Word of God as a powerful offensive weapon against spiritual attacks. Encourage teenagers to read and study the Bible regularly, memorize key verses, and use Scripture to combat negative thoughts or challenges they may face. While not part of the physical armor mentioned in Ephesians 6, prayer is emphasized as essential for staying connected to God and seeking His guidance and protection. Teach teenagers about the importance of prayer in building a relationship with God, seeking His will, and finding strength in times of need.

HOW GOD COMMUNICATES WITH YOU

God communicates with Teenagers in various ways, aiming to reach them in their unique stages of life and understanding. Understanding how God communicates with teenagers involves recognizing the complexities of their lives and the challenges they face. Here are some key ways through which God communicates with teenagers. The Bible serves as a primary source of communication from God to teenagers. Encouraging teens to read the Bible regularly can help them understand God's messages, teachings, and love for them. Prayer is a direct line of communication between individuals and God. Encouraging teenagers to pray regularly allows them to express their thoughts, feelings, and concerns to God while also listening for His guidance and responses. Many teenagers report feeling a sense of connection or communication with God during spiritual experiences such as worship services, retreats, or moments of reflection. These experiences can help reinforce their faith and sense of closeness to

God. Adults, mentors, or role models who embody Christian values can serve as channels through which teenagers receive guidance, advice, and wisdom that they perceive as coming from God. Some teenagers believe that God communicates with them through the events and circumstances of their lives. They may see signs or experience situations that they interpret as messages from God. The Holy Spirit is believed to work within individuals, including teenagers, guiding them towards truth, righteousness, and understanding. Teens may feel nudges or convictions in their hearts that they attribute to God's communication. Encouraging open dialogue about faith, providing opportunities for spiritual growth and exploration, and fostering a supportive environment where teens feel comfortable discussing their beliefs can all contribute to helping teenagers recognize and understand how God communicates with them.

WHO IS GOD

God, as described in the Bible, is the creator of the universe and all living beings. He is a loving and caring entity who sent His son, Jesus Christ, to Earth to offer salvation to humanity. God is often depicted as omnipotent, omniscient, and omnipresent, meaning He is all-powerful, all-knowing, and present everywhere at all times. For teenagers seeking to understand who God is, the Bible serves as the primary source of information about His character, attributes, and intentions towards humanity. In the Bible, particularly in passages like 1 John 4:9-10, God's love for humanity is emphasized. It highlights that God's love was demonstrated through the sacrifice of Jesus Christ for the forgiveness of sins. This act showcases God's immense love and compassion for His creation. Understanding God through Scripture is one of the best ways for teenagers to comprehend who God is through reading and studying the Bible. The Bible provides insights into God's nature, His interactions with humanity throughout history, and His plan for salvation. By delving into biblical passages that describe God's character and actions, teenagers can gain a deeper understanding of His love, mercy, justice, and grace. God's love and sacrifice is a central aspect of understanding who God is revolves around His unconditional love for humanity. The Bible teaches that God's love surpasses human comprehension and that He willingly sacrificed His son to redeem mankind from sin. This sacrificial act demonstrates God's selfless nature and desire for reconciliation with His creation.

WHAT GOD WANTS TEENS TO KNOW

God wants teenagers to know various important things according to the Bible. Here are some key points you should know concerning your life

1. Life is short and should not be wasted (James 4:14).
2. Following God's plan leads to a blessed life (Psalms 1:1).
3. Taking advantage of others robs oneself of character and dignity (Proverbs 28:24).
4. Your actions as a child will shape your reputation (Proverbs 20:11).
5. Authority in your life is valuable (Hebrews 13:17
6. Obedience to parents is important (Ephesians 6:2).
7. God will never forsake you, even if others do (Psalms 27:10).

8. A rebellious life leads to regrets (Proverbs 19:26).
9. Youth doesn't excuse sin; judgment awaits all (Ecclesiastes 11:9).
10. Bad choices can be forgiven by God (Psalms 25:7).

Concerning your salvation:

11. All have sinned and need salvation (Romans 5:12).
12. Remember God in youth for a meaningful testimony (Ecclesiastes 12:1).
13. Salvation is not limited by age; children are welcomed by Jesus (Matthew 19:14).
14. Keeping the commandments alone does not grant salvation (Matthew 19:20).
15. Salvation comes through Jesus alone (John 14:6).

Concerning your service for Him:

16. You can set an example for other youth in faith and conduct (1 Timothy 4:12).
17. God created you with a purpose in mind before birth (Jeremiah 1:5).

MESSAGE TO TEENS FROM GOD

1. **You are fearfully and wonderfully made:** Remember that you are created with great reverence and interest by God. You are unique and marvelous, just the way you are.
2. **God has a plan for your life:** Trust that God has a purpose for you, a future full of hope and promise. He will never leave you or fail you.
3. **Be strong and courageous:** Know that God goes with you, so do not be afraid or discouraged. You have the strength to face any challenges that come your way.
4. **You are loved unconditionally:** God's love for you is unconditional and everlasting. Embrace this love and let it guide you through both good and tough times.
5. **Seek wisdom in God's word:** Find guidance, comfort, and inspiration in the Bible. Let the

words of scripture uplift you and give you strength.

6. **Embrace your uniqueness:** Celebrate your individuality and the gifts that God has bestowed upon you. You are special in His eyes, just as you are.

7. **Trust in God's timing:** Even when things seem uncertain or difficult, trust that God's timing is perfect. He has a plan for your life that will unfold in due time.

8. **Find peace in prayer:** Turn to prayer as a source of comfort and solace. Pour out your heart to God, knowing that He listens and cares for you deeply.

9. **Be kind to yourself:** Treat yourself with the same kindness and compassion that God shows towards you. Forgive yourself, learn from mistakes, and grow stronger each day.

10. **Remember that you are never alone:** In moments of loneliness or despair, know that God is always by your side, ready to offer His love, guidance, and support.

THE IMPORTANCE OF PRAYER

Daily prayers can be particularly beneficial for teenagers as they help establish a sense of trust and comfort within themselves, allowing them to stay resilient during challenging times and nurture their emotional well-being. Here are some prayer ideas that teenagers can incorporate into their daily lives. Morning prayers provide an excellent opportunity for teenagers to start their day with a positive mindset and express gratitude for the blessings in their lives. Here's a sample morning prayer:

> **Dear God,** I thank you for this new day and the opportunities it brings. I am grateful for my family, friends, and teachers who have made a difference in my life. Please guide me today, giving me strength, courage, and wisdom to make the right decisions. Amen.

EVENING PRAYERS

Evening prayers allow teenagers to reflect on their day, express gratitude for positive experiences, and seek guidance for any challenges they may have faced. Here's a sample evening prayer:

> **Loving God,** Thank you for being with me throughout this day. I am grateful for the moments of joy and the lessons learned from difficulties. Please help me remember your presence in every moment of my life, so that I may follow your path with joy and enthusiasm. Amen.

DEVOTIONAL PRAYERS

Reading religious texts or devotionals can help deepen teenagers' understanding of their faith while encouraging mindfulness and reflection. Here's a sample devotional prayer:

Gracious God, I ask you to reveal yourself to me through these words (reading from religious text or devotional). Help me understand your message and apply it to my life so that I may grow closer to you each day. Amen.

WALKING IN THE FRUITS OF THE SPIRIT

Love

Bible Reading: John 15:12-13
Explanation: Love is foundational in the Christian faith. It involves sacrificially putting others' needs above your own, as Jesus taught to love God and others.

Joy

Bible Reading: Philippians 4:4
Explanation: Joy is a deep contentment rooted in knowing and trusting God, not dependent on circumstances but on God's unchanging love.

Peace

Bible Reading: Colossians 3:15
Explanation: Peace is the calm assurance from trusting in God's control and sovereignty, finding rest in His presence even in uncertain times.

Patience

Bible Reading: James 1:2-4
Explanation: Patience is enduring difficulties without giving up, trusting in God's timing and plan even when it seems unclear.

Kindness

Bible Reading: Ephesians 4:32
Explanation: Kindness is treating others with compassion and respect, going out of your way to help them even if it inconveniences you.

Goodness

Bible Reading: Romans 12:21
Explanation: Goodness is pursuing moral excellence and integrity, doing what is right even when challenging or unpopular.

Faithfulness

Bible Reading: Hebrews 10:23
Explanation: Faithfulness is remaining true to your word and faith, even when faced with challenges or doubt.

ACKNOWLEDGEMENT

I would like to thank my dad, Carl, and my sisters, India, Kindia,(Billy) Glendia, April, my nieces Kaliah and Rose for their unwavering support. Their love, encouragement, and presence in my life have been amazing. I am truly blessed to have such a wonderful family who stands by me through thick and thin.

Dad has always been my rock, offering guidance and wisdom whenever I needed it. His unconditional love and support have shaped me into the person I am today. I am grateful for his sacrifices and the lessons he has taught me along the way.

My sisters India, Kindia, Glendia, April have been my pillars of strength. Their constant support, understanding, and companionship have brought immense joy to my life. Whether it's sharing laughter or wiping away tears, they have always been there for me.

I want to thank my uncles Edward, Adam and all my family and friends for being a source of comfort and inspiration. Their presence in my life is a gift that I cherish every day. I am grateful for the bond we share and the memories we create together. My extended sisters Nina, Realitea, Mariah, Kamya. Special thank to everyone who supported me.

In loving memories of Xzavier Thompson. I love and miss you!

TO MY MOTHER

I would like to express my deepest gratitude to my God and my mother for her unwavering support and encouragement throughout the process of writing this book. Her love, guidance, and belief in me have been invaluable, and I am truly grateful for everything she has done to help me bring this project to fruition.

From the very beginning, my mother has been my rock, always there to listen to my ideas, provide feedback, and offer words of encouragement when I needed them most. Her unwavering faith in my abilities has been a source of strength for me, pushing me to overcome challenges and persevere through moments of doubt.

Throughout the long hours spent researching, writing, and editing this book, my mother has been by my side every step of the way. Whether it was staying up late to help me brainstorm ideas or offering a shoulder to lean on during moments of frustration, her support has been unwavering and unconditional.

I am truly blessed to have a mother who believes in me wholeheartedly and who has shown me what it means to pursue your passions with dedication and perseverance. This book would not have been possible without her love, guidance, and unwavering support, and for that, I am eternally grateful for my mom and especially my Lord and savior Jesus Christ.

ADVICE FROM THE AUTHOR

As a 17-year-old, here are some advice that I would offer to other teenagers based on my own experiences and observations. I had to learn how to embrace my uniqueness and individuality. Don't try to fit in or change who you are just to please others. Authenticity is key to building genuine relationships and finding true happiness. Choose friends who uplift you, support you, and bring out the best in you. Avoid toxic relationships that drain your energy and self-esteem. Your circle of friends plays a significant role in shaping your mindset and behaviors. Take care of your physical, mental, and emotional well-being. Make time for activities that recharge you, whether it's reading this book, going for a walk, or practicing mindfulness. Self-care is not selfish it's essential for maintaining overall health. Understand that making mistakes is a natural part of growth. Instead of being afraid of failure, see it as an opportunity to learn, improve, and become resilient. Don't be too hard on yourself when things don't go as planned. Define your aspirations and set achievable goals to work towards them. Whether it's academic success, personal development, or pursuing a passion, having clear objectives can give you direction and motivation. Don't hesitate to reach out for help when you're struggling with mental health issues, academic challenges, or personal problems. Talk to trusted adults, school counselors, or mental health professionals who can provide support and guidance. Cultivate a mindset of gratitude by appreciating the positive aspects of your life, no matter how small they may seem. Gratitude can boost your mood, enhance your relationships, and foster resilience during tough times. Be open to new experiences, ideas, and perspectives. Curiosity fuels personal growth and intellectual development. Explore different interests, hobbies, and subjects that spark your curiosity. While social media can be a valuable tool for connection and information sharing, it's essential to maintain a healthy balance in its usage. Limit screen time, prioritize real-life interactions, and be mindful of the impact of social media on your self-esteem. Have confidence in your abilities and potential. Trust yourself to overcome challenges, adapt to changes, and pursue your dreams with determination, resilience and put God first in your life.

THE PRAYER

Heavenly Father,

We come before You today with humble hearts, recognizing the weight of our actions and the state of our world. We acknowledge our shortcomings—both as individuals and as a nations—and we seek Your forgiveness. We ask that You instill in us a spirit of repentance, guiding us to turn away from paths that lead to division, hatred, and injustice.

Lord, we pray for the leaders of this world. Grant them wisdom beyond their years; let them be vessels of Your truth. May they stand firm on the core values of integrity and honesty, ensuring that their decisions reflect fairness and justice for all people—regardless of race, creed, or status. Inspire them to prioritize the welfare of their citizens over personal gain or political ambition.

We beseech You to open their eyes to the suffering around them. Let compassion guide their hearts so they may recognize the dignity inherent in every human life.

May they work tirelessly towards policies that uplift the marginalized and provide opportunities for those in need.

Father, we ask that You bless our communities with unity and understanding. Help us to listen more than we speak; may we build bridges instead of walls. Let love be our guiding principle as we engage with one another in dialogue aimed at healing rather than harming.

As we repent for our past mistakes—individually and collectively—we pray for strength to make amends where possible. Empower us to take action against injustice in all its forms, standing up not only for ourselves but also for those who cannot stand up for themselves.

May Your light shine upon us as we navigate these turbulent times. Let it illuminate paths toward peace and reconciliation among nations torn apart by conflict. Instill in leaders a sense of accountability; remind them that true leadership is rooted in service rather than power.

Finally, Lord, we ask that You grant us patience as we await change. Help us remember that transformation often takes time but is always possible through faith and perseverance.

In Your holy name, we pray, Amen.

www.ingramcontent.com/pod-product-compliance
Lightning Source LLC
LaVergne TN
LVHW011841060526
838200LV00054B/4123